THE LOVE CHALLENGE

30 DAYS, 30 WAYS
To Increase The Love
In Your Relationship

MELISSA DUMAZ, LMFT

Copyright 2018

All rights reserved. No part of this book may be reproduced or transmitted in any form or by any means, electronic or mechanical, including photocopying, recording, or by an information stored in a retrieval system without written permission from the author, except for the inclusion of brief quotes in a review.

Melissa Dumaz, MS, LMFT

The Love Challenge: 30 Days, 30 Ways To Increase The Love In Your Relationship

Edited by: Paper Raven Books

Published by: U Help You

Paperback ISBN= 978-1-7323104-0-7

Hardback ISBN= 978-1-7323104-1-4

Printed in the United States of America

I would like to dedicate this book to my dear husband. It is his love and his love for me that has truly challenged me to love and grow in ways that I have never experienced before. B.D. I love you with all of me. Thank you for showing me what unconditional love looks like in the earthly form. You truly are a blessing from God, and I am beyond blessed to share this life with you. When I look at our children, I can't help but feel excited knowing that it is our love for each other and God's love for us that created our three beautiful blessings. Team Dumaz ALWAYS!

To my children, Mommy loves you. Love moves us, transforms us, and bonds us. Please always remember that all we do should be done in love.

To my mother and my sister, thank you for believing in me, for encouraging me, and for reminding me that God placed this book in me and that He wanted me to see it through.

To my mother in-law (rest well) & father in-law, thank you. Thank you for welcoming me into the family with open arms. Thank you for loving me as your daughter. Thank you for showing us the joys and the blessings of what 50 years of marriage looks like. And, most of all, thank you for raising an outstanding man who I feel so blessed and grateful to call my husband.

Table Of Contents

Introduction	1
Day 1: Your Commitment to Begin	3
Day 2: Speak Words of Love into Your Relationship	7
Day 3: A Heart of Gratitude	11
Day 4: Love Notes	15
Day 5: Game Night	19
Day 6: I-Statements	23
Day 7: Love Challenge Reflection: Week #1	29
Day 8: Let Us Pray	33
Day 9: Pillow Talk	37
Day 10: Fighting Fair	41
Day 11: Make a Proper Apology	51
Day 12: Random Acts of Kindness	55
Day 13: Date Night	59
Day 14 : Love Challenge Reflection: Week #2	63
Day 15: Say It with a Song	67
Day 16: The Power of Touch	71
Day 17: Appreciation List	75
Day 18: Appreciation List Delivery	79

Day 19: Give a Gift	83
Day 20: Delete Your Records	87
Day 21: Love Challenge Reflection: Week #3	91
Day 22: Love Language	95
Day 23: Faithfulness	99
Day 24: Team Us	103
Day 25: Remember When We Met	107
Day 26: Bring Chivalry Back	111
Day 27: Mission Statement	115
Day 28: Love Challenge Reflection: Week #4	121
Day 29: Your Vision, Your Goals	125
Day 30: Commitments	131
Day 31: Let's Celebrate Love	135
Reflections of the Love Challenge	139
Declarations	141
About the Author	145

Introduction

Hello. Welcome to The Love Challenge! You most likely picked up this book because you're looking for ways to restore, reignite, or replenish the love in your relationship. I want you to know that you have come to the right place.

This Love Challenge is about refreshing a love that is already present, adding new tools to express your love for your significant other, and improving the foundation on which you have built your relationship. This Love Challenge can be used in addition to couple's counseling; however, please be advised that it is not a substitute for counseling and cannot take the place of a relationship with a licensed mental health professional.

The Love Challenge was developed to be completed in a month—one challenge per day for the next thirty days—but I challenge you to make these practices a part of your relationship every day, to re-visit these chapters as needed, and to re-do the daily practices as often as your relationship desires and requires.

Some of the daily challenges require some planning and preparation. I believe that you can get the most of out of this book by reading the challenge of the day the night before. This reading tip can help you feel prepared to work toward completing the challenge as soon as you get up in the morning.

Single readers, don't worry, I didn't forget about you! I encourage you to do this Love Challenge for yourself or for anyone in your life you love (mom, dad, sister, brother, friend). There's always room to love better and there's no harm in taking care of YOU by loving YOU better. Some of the Love Challenges will absolutely require modification, but you are encouraged to join in for this 30 day (plus a bonus day) Love Challenge.

Are you ready for your transformation?

Please feel free to join The Love Challenge Facebook page, 30 Day Love Challenge and share your journey with others!

You may also share your experiences with the daily challenges on your social media pages to encourage your friends and family to join. Use hashtags #ChallengeYourLove and #LoveChallengeByMel to share your journey. Thank you.

YOUR COMMITMENT TO BEGIN

DAY 1

Let's talk about LOVE and how to challenge yours to be better. It's only natural that when you are considering change, you start thinking about the goals you have set for yourself in the past. It's typical to set goals for weight, finances, and career, but what about love? What about relationships? Self-improvement is good, but relationship-improvement is great! What are your relationship goals? Are you willing to challenge yourself daily to improve your relationship?

The Love Challenge is a daily practice that I have created to increase, enhance, nurture, grow, and improve the love in your life between you and your significant other. If your relationship is great, I pray that this challenge will be the icing on the cake. If your relationship is good, I pray that this challenge will be the tune-up that you need. If your relationship is strained, I pray that this challenge will rehabilitate and assist in transforming your love to be outstanding!

The Love Challenge

Every day for the next 30 days, I encourage you to complete a Love Challenge throughout the day. The true challenge will be stepping outside of your comfort zone, taking yourself off of auto-pilot, and engaging in the daily tasks of love. This challenge is set up to be done by you. It does not require that your significant other do it with you, but of course the two of you can do the challenge together. The main goal is that this challenge will enhance the love in your relationship and stretch you to love better. The bonus is that hopefully your significant other will see the change in you and that you both will be transformed.

Love is bold. Love takes courage. Today's challenge is your commitment to engage in The Love Challenge for 30 days! Are you in?

Speak Words of Love into Your Relationship

DAY 2

Today, I challenge you to speak words of love into your relationship. Words are powerful! I encourage you to use words of kindness (even during an argument) and to be respectful with your significant other, following the simple rule: "if you don't have anything nice to say, don't say anything at all." Negative interactions, big and small, with the one you love can eventually permeate your relationship. Refrain from negative statements, including sarcasm and undermining comments, and especially statements that may make the one you love feel uncared for.

Tell your loved one how important they are to you. Communicate your feelings openly. Be honest. Your words should build up your relationship, not tear it down. Think before you speak. Limit the negativity. Make sure your words are genuine. If you slip, stop and start again.

Already speaking words of love into your relationship? I challenge you to kick it up a notch! Here are a few examples to get you started:

The Love Challenge

1. You make me happy.
2. I am so grateful to have you in my life.
3. You make me better.
4. I want to grow old with you.
5. You bring out the best in me.
6. You are everything that I want in a partner.
7. I appreciate you.
8. I love you.
9. You are perfect for me.
10. I love doing life with you.

A Heart of Gratitude

DAY 3

Melissa Dumaz

Today, I challenge you to have and maintain a heart of gratitude. It's easy to get stuck in mundane routines: wake up, get dressed, go to work, cook, clean, and shower, only to sleep and wake to do the same thing all over again, day in and day out. Routine can also desensitize you to all the things and the people you should be thankful for. Auto-pilot kicks in, and you forget to thank your spouse for taking out the trash, cooking, cleaning, doing laundry, and working hard for the family. Today, I want you to thank your spouse for EVERYTHING they do today for you, your kids, and your family. Thank them for the big things, the small things, and even for the things that are their "duty." Just say, "Thank You."

A grateful heart does not complain or compare. A grateful heart does not grumble or gripe. Having a grateful heart will fill you and your spouse up, and it will make you and your spouse want to keep giving to each other. Your gratitude toward your loved one can be spoken in words, or it can be shown in actions. A grateful heart is beautiful and gives mutually to both the giver and receiver.

There are many ways to look for gratitude in your everyday life. If you're having a hard time finding it, you can start with being grateful for the breath you are breathing right now. Be grateful for the person you have in your life who has inspired you to challenge your love to make it better. You can keep a gratitude journal by writing down all the things that you are grateful for daily. You can also start a Good Stuff Jar in your home and keep a list of all the things you and your family are grateful for.

Filling your heart with gratitude can be as easy as taking a few minutes when you first wake up and before you fall asleep, to acknowledge the things and the people you are grateful for.

Thank you for participating in The Love Challenge, thank you for reading this book, and thank you for your commitment to love better. In that alone, my heart is filled.

"Gratitude… turns what we have into enough and more. It turns denial into acceptance, chaos to order, confusion to clarity. It can turn a meal into a feast, a house into a home, a stranger into a friend. Gratitude makes sense of our past, brings peace for today and creates a vision for tomorrow."– Melody Beattie

Love Notes

DAY 4

Melissa Dumaz

Today, I challenge you to write a handwritten love note to your significant other. A note is a romantic way to express feelings of love, not in a text message, email, or social media post but in a genuine pen-to-paper love note. You can hand deliver the love note to your significant other, you can mail it, or you can strategically put it in a place where they will find it and read it in private. A few suggestions on where you can place it: tucked in their lunch box, taped to the steering wheel of their car, or propped against the bathroom mirror. Use this time to be creative!

I encourage you to include in your love note an expression of your love and one thing that you appreciate about him or her. The love note for today's challenge will be a simple but heartfelt one.

The Love Challenge

Dear Lover,

I love you. I really appreciate you for providing for and protecting our family.

Sincerely,

Your Lover

xo

GAME NIGHT

DAY 5

Today, I challenge you to have a Game Night with your significant other. You've been working hard all week, and tonight you can take some time and simply enjoy your loved one. Pick a game or two, pour a glass of wine, prepare your favorite snacks, and have a good time with one another tonight. If your significant other works tonight or if you have a prior engagement and cannot do game night tonight, then I challenge you to schedule a game night. Find an evening when both of you are free, put it on the calendar, add a reminder to each other's phone, and make it happen! If you have children and decide to include them in the game night, make sure you save a round for just you and your significant other after the kids have gone to bed. While it's great to include children in the fun, strengthening the relationship between mother and father comes first!

Game night is the perfect way to enjoy each other's company and create intimacy while staying within a budget. You can spend the evening laughing, sharing stories, and focusing on strengthening your relationship.

What's your favorite game? Here are some game suggestions:

Apples to Apples®

Dominoes™

Uno®

Scrabble®

Mancala

Chess

Pictionary®

Checkers

Jenga®

Backgammon

Boggle®

For a spark of romance, you can even play Strip Poker! Whatever you decide, have fun!

I-Statements

DAY 6

Melissa Dumaz

Today I challenge you to make I-Statements. Good communication is imperative in any relationship, and accepting responsibility for your feelings is one of the most important communication skills you can gain. This form of communication may be new to you, and it may make take some time to become comfortable with it. Practice, practice, practice. If you mess up, that's okay! Just keep practicing, and over time it will start to feel like second nature.

What is an I-Statement?

An I-Statement consists of a description of how you feel, what has made you feel that way, and an explanation of why. You can also take the I-Statement one step further and share what you would like the other person to do differently.

For example: *I feel* (state what you are feeling) *when you* (describe the other person's behavior or what has made you feel the way you feel), *because* (explain why the other person's behavior has caused you to feel this way). For instance, *I feel annoyed when you don't give me your full attention when I am talking to you, because I then have to repeat myself several times, and I get the impression from you that what I have to say is not important.*

Taking it one step further would include a statement about changes you would like to see from the other person: *I would like it if you would* (state what you would like the person to do differently). For instance, *I feel annoyed when you don't give me your full attention when I am talking to you, because I then have to repeat myself several times, and I get the impression from you that what I have to say is not important. I would like it if you would give me your undivided attention when I am talking to you, or let me know when would be a good time to have each other's undivided attention.*

A great time to use an I-Statement is when you have a problem with someone or something. I-Statements can provide a less hostile form of communication and can assist with minimizing blaming others for our feelings. We do ourselves and our loved ones a disservice when we blame others for making us feel the way we do. An I-Statement can also assist in decreasing communication that leads to defensiveness. For example, it helps to avoid statements such as, "You make me so angry!" "You are inconsiderate!" and "You shut up!" A more productive way to communicate those feelings would be, "I feel angry when you… because…" and so on.

Remember, an I-Statement has three parts (or four parts if you can go one step further*). Here is your cheat sheet to assist with making proper I-Statements:

1. The Emotion: *I feel…*

2. The Behavior: *When you…*

3. The Why: *Because…*

4. *The Change: *I would like…*

I have also included a list of feelings words to get you started. Feel free to add your own feelings words to that list!

Feelings Words Vocabulary

Happy	Disgusted	Mad	Sad	Scared
Adored	Embarrassed	Anger	Apathetic	Afraid
Alive	Fed up	Agitated	Ashamed	Anxious
Appreciated	Grossed out	Animosity	Bewildered	Cautious
Cheerful	Guilty	Bitter	Blue	Cowardly
Ecstatic	Ignored	Defensive	Defeated	Fearful
Elated	Inadequate	Defiant	Despair	Helpless
Excited	Incompetent	Disturbed	Despondent	Hesitant
Glad	Inept	Enraged	Discouraged	Insecure
Grateful	Inferior	Frustrated	Distracted	Irrational
Hopeful	Insignificant	Hostile	Disturbed	Petrified
Jolly	Repelled	Infuriated	Down	Powerless
Joyful	Repulsed	Intolerant	Heavyhearted	Provoked
Loved	Shame	Irrational	Hopeless	Reluctant
Merry	Sick	Irritated	Hurt	Resentful
Optimistic	Sick and tired	Livid	Inferior	Startled
Pleased	Stupid	Mad	Insecure	Suspicious
Satisfied	Turned off	Outraged	Irrational	Terrified
Terrific	Ugly	Provoked	Lonely	Unsafe
Thankful	Unaccepted	Reluctant	Misunderstood	Unsure
Thrilled	Unhappy	Revengeful	Overwhelmed	Vulnerable
Uplifted	Upset	Stubborn	Sorry	Worried

Love Challenge Reflection: Week #1

DAY 7

Melissa Dumaz

Congratulations, you have made it through your first week of the Love Challenge! So far, you have made a commitment to join and complete The Love Challenge, you have spoken words of love, you have committed to have a heart of gratitude, you wrote a love note, you scheduled a game night, and you have been practicing I-Statements. It's been a fantastic week!

Today, I challenge you to review the first week. I encourage you to take this time to reflect on how the first week has been going for YOU. Are you having fun? Have you felt challenged? If you find yourself struggling with a day's challenge, don't give up. Just keep practicing. I don't expect you to gain all of this overnight. However, I do encourage you to press on, to step out of your comfort zone, and to continue practicing and implementing the daily challenges. If there's a particular challenge that comes naturally to you, great! Simply use this time to do more of it.

As a gentle reminder, the focus here is YOU: YOU loving better and YOU doing your part to improve your relationship. It's easy to become discouraged if you are working on yourself and do not get the desired response from others. Don't be discouraged. Keep loving. Persevere in transforming YOUR heart. Go into these challenges with an open heart and avoid completing a day challenge just to mark it off the list. If there was a label on the side of the Love Challenge, it would read: open mind and open heart required!

Please feel free to join The Love Challenge Facebook page, 30 Day Love Challenge to share your week one challenges and triumphs. Thank you all so very much! May your week be off to a great start full of love and bountiful blessings.

Let Us Pray

DAY 8

Melissa Dumaz

Today, I challenge you to pray for your significant other, not as a plea to make up for what they lack but as a recognition of all they bring to your life. The words you pray can be powerful and effective in your life. If you're already doing this, then continue to do so and simply add an extra prayer for today. Prayer is not only beneficial for the one being prayed for; it is also good for the one doing the praying.

If you're looking to kick this specific challenge up a notch, you can ask your significant other to pray with you. Again, if you're already doing this, then continue to do so and simply add an extra prayer for today. If you're not already praying with your loved one and would like to begin, here's a way to get started:

1. Pick a time and a place where you will be free of distractions.

2. Hold hands (you can sit or stand facing one another).

3. Each take a turn to share your prayer requests.

4. One of you pray aloud including both of your prayer requests.

5. Once you are done, spend some time physically embracing one another.

Praying with one another in this manner is a great way to spend time together. It enhances your intimacy with one another and your intimacy with God, by allowing for open sharing of the matters of your heart. It also strengthens your relationship together and your relationship with God, and can be the glue that binds the two of you together.

Start with a short prayer until you get used to praying for your loved one. Ask God to bring healing and growth to your relationship, and thank God for your significant other. Lastly, remember that prayer is simply talking to God; don't be afraid to pour out your heart. I pray that your love will be transformed. Amen.

Pillow Talk

DAY
9

Today, I challenge you to go to bed at the same time as your significant other and have some pillow talk. Pillow talk is a great way to enjoy each other's presence through conversation. Your pillow talk can be silly, sweet, or a time to clear your minds. It is not a time to argue or fight (save that for another time!). During pillow talk, you can ask your loved one about their life dreams, their goals, what brings them joy, and anything else your heart desires.

Your daily routine and lifestyle may present barriers that make it difficult for you to go to bed at the same time as your loved one. Remember, The Love Challenge requires you to get out of your comfort zone, to make some sacrifices, and to do some things differently so that you get different results! Here is troubleshooting for some common scenarios that may make pillow talk a challenge:

- Significant other working late? Set your alarm to wake up when they get home.

- Significant other working nightshift? Have pillow talk via Skype, FaceTime, or the phone before bedtime.

- Significant other goes to bed too early or too late? Well, for tonight you do too! Or you can ask your loved one to adjust their bedtime for you tonight.

- Significant other upset and doesn't want to talk? That's okay. You can do most of the talking. You can also ask most of the questions during pillow talk.

Enjoy your pillow talk, and sweet dreams!

Fighting Fair

DAY 10

Melissa Dumaz

Today, I challenge you to make a commitment to fight fair. Every couple argues, and it's natural for different viewpoints to lead to conflict in relationships. However, arguments can be constructive if you implement some rules for fighting fair. Some of the benefits of fighting fair include shorter arguments, less intense conflicts, and happier endings.

Below, you will find a list of dirty fighting techniques. Take a moment to identify which of these techniques you are currently using. Once you learn your dirty fighting techniques, write them on a piece of paper and then throw them in the trash! Today, you commit to fight fair, and the first step to fighting fair is to stop fighting dirty.

Dirty Fighting Techniques[1]

1. *Timing.* Pick the right time to begin an argument. Late at night, during a favorite TV show, after several drinks, or just before your spouse has to leave for work are options. As a general rule, look for the time your spouse least expects it or is least able to respond.

2. *Escalating.* Move quickly from the issue, to questioning of personality, to wondering whether it is worth the effort to stay together (issue to personality to relationship). Interpret your spouse's shortcomings as evidence of bad faith and the impossibility of a happy relationship.

3. *Brown Bagging.* Try to list as many problems in as much detail as possible. Don't stick to the original issue, but rather throw in all the problems you can think of. Don't limit yourself to the present. If your partner can't recall the offense, all the better.

4. *Overgeneralizing.* Use words like "always" and "never" as in, "You are always late." This is likely to distract your partner into discussing the overgeneralization rather than the issue and insure further misunderstandings.

5. *Cross-Complaining.* Respond to any complaint your spouse may raise with one of your own. For example, "Me late? Why, if it weren't for the fact that you never

---

[1] The original author of the Dirty Fighting Techniques #1-28 is currently unknown. If you are the original author of these techniques please contact The Love Challenge author as soon as possible; so that proper credit can be given for your work. Thank you.

have any clean clothes for me..." If done properly, you can balance complaint against complaint forever.

6. *Crucializing.* Exaggerate the importance of the issue with statements such as, "If you really loved us, you would never have done it in the first place," or, "This proves that you don't care." Never concede that an issue is not absolutely critical and in need of immediate resolution.

7. *Asking Why.* "Why didn't you clean up?" or "Why were you late?" will imply that there must be something terribly wrong with your spouse and that something more than an easily resolved, simple problem behavior is at issue.

8. *Blaming.* Make it clear that the fault lies entirely with your spouse and that once again, you are simply the innocent victim. Don't admit that your behavior plays any part in the difficulty. Make sure your spouse realizes that you will not change first.

9. *Pulling Rank.* Rather than depend on the merits of your argument, pull rank by reminding your partner that you make more money, have more education, are older or younger, or are wiser or more experienced in such matters. Anything that will enhance your status at your spouse's expense should be considered.

10. *Not Listening, Dominating.* Any time you appear to be listening, you run the risk of suggesting that you value your partner's opinion. Talk while your spouse is talking, pretend to read, or even fall asleep.

11. *Listing Injustices.* This is a great morale builder. By reciting every slight injustice or inequity you have suffered in the relationship, you will experience a renewed sense of self- righteousness. You can use this approach to justify almost any activity you have always wanted to engage in. For example, "Since you went ahead and bought that dress, I can buy a new car."

12. *Labeling.* By labeling somebody in a negative manner, you can create the impression that person is totally at fault. Psychological labels, such as "childish," "neurotic," "insecure," or "alcoholic," are particularly effective in obscuring issues where you may be vulnerable.

13. *Mind-reading.* By deciding that you know the *real* reason why someone is acting in a certain way, you can avoid having to debate issues. For example, "You only said that to set me up," or, "You don't really feel that way," are particularly effective.

14. *Fortune-Telling.* Predicting the future can save you the effort of really trying to resolve problems. "You will never change," or, "It would be easy for me to change, but you won't live up to it," are statements that can protect you from having to make any efforts at all.

15. *Being Sarcastic.* This is a great way of saying something without having to take responsibility for it. If you can say, "You're so smart..." just right, you can imply that your spouse is stupid and deny that you said it at the same time.

16. *Avoiding Responsibility.* Although not a very elegant tactic, saying, "I don't remember," can bring the discussion to an abrupt halt. Alcohol or fatigue can serve the same purpose, as in, "I must have been drunk."

17. *Leaving.* No problem is so big or important that it can't be ignored. Walk out of the room, leave home, or just refuse to talk. Sometimes just threatening to leave can accomplish the same ends without the inconvenience involved in actually leaving.

18. *Rejecting Compromise.* Don't back down. Why settle for compromise when with a little luck you can really devastate your spouse (and destroy the relationship). Stick with the "one winner" philosophy.

19. *Personalizing.* Anybody can resolve a conflict by sticking to the issue. Shift to personalities and you should be able to generate enough defensiveness to keep the conflict going forever.

20. *Playing the Martyr.* If timed properly, this tactic can completely disorient the opposition. "You're right dear, I am hopeless," can stop your spouse cold. An example of a less subtle form is, "How could you say that after all I've done for you?" An extreme form is to threaten to kill yourself if your spouse doesn't shape up.

21. *Using Money.* "If you made as much money as..." or, "When you make as much as I do, then you can have an opinion," are old favorites.

22. *Using Children.* "If you spent more time with them, they wouldn't be failing," or, "Do you want them to grow up like you?" can always be used unless you are so unfortunate as to have perfect children.

23. *Using Relatives.* "When you do that, you are just like your mother," can be used to break your spouse's concentration and undermine confidence.

24. *Giving Advice.* By telling people how to act, think, and feel, you can maintain a position of superiority while insisting that you are only trying to be helpful.

25. *Getting Even.* Don't settle for a compromise or an apology. Hold grudges for as long as possible; you might need those complaints in future arguments.

26. *Using Terminal Language.* For example, if you happen to be upset by the fact that the room wasn't straightened, start with "you slob…" to suggest that it is your spouse's existence and not behavior that is at question.

27. *Being Inconsistent.* Keep your spouse off balance by changing your position. Try complaining that your spouse never talks to you, and then ignore whatever your spouse says.

28. *Others.* This list should only be considered suggestive of the range of tactics to be drawn from. With patience and creativity, you should be able to come up with numerous innovations.

After you have identified which dirty fighting techniques you tend to use, sit with your loved one and set up some rules for arguing, such as: no name calling, no walking out on each other, no foul language used toward one another, and no telling the other to "shut up." It's your relationship; you can set the rules! Remember that rules only work if you follow them. Once the new rules are set, both parties have to agree and make changes accordingly.

Lastly, as it's been mentioned on other Day Challenges, change does not always happen overnight. If you slip, stop and start again. If your loved one slips, gently remind them of the rules, forgive, and start again.

Cheers to fighting fair!

*Fighting in this chapter refers specifically to verbal and non-verbal arguments. Physical violence, especially domestic violence,[2] is never part of a healthy relationship. Domestic violence is a serious matter that can result in death. If you or someone you know is being abused, please seek help and safety as soon as possible! Call the National Domestic Violence Hotline at 1-800-799-7233 or visit their site at http://www.thehotline.org/help/

---

[2] Domestic violence is abuse that happens in a personal relationship. It can happen between past or current partners, spouses, and boyfriends or girlfriends. This type of violence affects men and women of any ethnic group, race, or religion; gay or straight; rich or poor; teen, adult, or elderly. The abuser may use fear, bullying, and threats to gain power and control over another individual.

Make a Proper Apology

DAY 11

Today, I challenge you to make a proper apology. Yesterday, you were challenged to stop fighting dirty and to identify ways that you have fought dirty in the past with your loved one. Now that you are aware of how you fight dirty, go and make a proper apology and a commitment to no longer fight that way. If there's nothing new to apologize for, then apologize for something you have yet to apologize for. This is not to rehash old wounds; rather, a heartfelt apology can clean and bring closure to many wounds.

Raise your hand if you have a hard time apologizing (I'm raising my hand). One of the most important things you can do for your relationship is to make a proper apology as needed. Humility brings wisdom. Simply hoping things will just get better, ignoring problems, sweeping things under the rug, and allowing tensions to build up, only weighs your relationship down. Lift some of the dead weight from your relationship by making a good and proper apology.

Saying, "I'm sorry," just isn't enough. An apology is an expression of regret for something that you have done wrong. The formula for a proper apology is: *I apologize for* (state what you are apologizing for), *I will not do* (state what you will not do again) *again. Do you forgive me?*

Once you've made your genuine apology, the next move is up to your loved one. If your apology is not well received, but you were genuine in giving your apology, don't worry; your loved one may just need more time. If you are on the receiving end of an apology, then forgiveness is up to you. To forgive means to stop feeling anger and resentment toward the one who wronged you. Anger and resentment can lead to spite and bitterness. Remember, you do not forgive for the sake of the other person. You forgive to heal yourself. Once you receive an apology from your loved one, let them know they are forgiven. A simple "I forgive you" is all that is needed.

Now, let's put all of that together in a scenario of Jack and Jill:

Jack: Jill, I apologize for raising my voice and walking out on you when we were arguing last night. I will not yell at you, and I will not walk out on you again. Do you forgive me?

Jill: Thank you, Jack, for your apology. Thank you for agreeing to speak to each other calmly and to stick it out even during conversations that are not easy to have. I forgive you.

Today, swallow your pride, give yourself permission to be vulnerable, go apologize, ask forgiveness, and forgive. You and your loved one deserve it.

Random Acts of Kindness

DAY 12

Today, I challenge you to perform a random act of kindness for your loved one. I want you to make a deliberate attempt to brighten your loved one's day by doing something thoughtful, nice, and caring for them. The biggest obstacle will be completing today's challenge, regardless of the condition of the relationship with your loved one at the present moment. Keep your heart and your intentions pure.

Here are a few examples:

- Surprise your loved one with lunch at the office today.

- Do your loved one's chores tonight.

- Give your loved one the night off from kitchen duties, kid duties, or cooking duties.

- Give your loved one a massage.

- Do your loved one a favor.

- Cook your loved one's favorite food or dessert.

- Surprise your loved one with their favorite coffee or smoothie.

Be mindful that these acts are to be random, kind, thoughtful, nice, and caring. You are not allowed to keep record of what you did for your loved one, nor are you allowed to use it or hold it against them later. This is a time to open your heart and allow your kindness to shine. You can even double-challenge yourself to do so many random acts of kindness today that you forget how many you did!

Kindness is contagious. Allow your kindness to be so great that it inspires someone else to be kind and creates a ripple effect.

Date Night

DAY 13

Tonight, I challenge you to a date night with your loved one. So far this week, you have been challenged to humble yourself and to step out of your box. It's time to take a deep breath and have some fun!

Date night is an arranged date and time to spend with your loved one, to reconnect with fun and romance. Especially if you have children, you may be long overdue for a date night. If you do not have a babysitter or date night funds, that's okay; you can arrange your date night to be at home after the kids go to bed. If your loved one is busy tonight, that's okay, too. Use today to schedule and plan a date night with your loved one and put it on the calendar. Prioritizing time for a fun date night is essential!

Your date night does not have to cost you money. I repeat, your date night does not have to cost you money. There are plenty of ways to enjoy each other's company doing what you two delight in, or trying something different on the town or at home.

Some suggestions for date night on the town include: lunch, dinner, movie, couples massage, cooking class, wine tasting, bowling, picnic, dancing or dance classes, comedy club, concert, live band, painting class, sports game, that one place you've been wanting to try, or that one thing your loved one has been wanting to do.

Date night at home can be very creative and fun as well. If you have children, date night can take place after you put the children to bed. Some suggestions include: order dinner or lunch in, breakfast in bed, a glass of wine, your favorite music playlist and dancing in your living room, rent a movie, watch your favorite movie together, light candles, make s'mores by the fireplace, make cocktails and appetizers, heat the pool or jacuzzi and take a night swim, take turns giving each other a massage, or play a game to learn more about one another.

Use this list as a starting place to get your wheels turning for ideas on how to be creative and freshen things up! Tonight's date should be about fun, romance, friendship, and growing closer. Use this time to rediscover one another. Leave the worries behind while on your date. Start planning NOW!

Love Challenge Reflection: Week #2

Day 14

Melissa Dumaz

Congratulations, you have made it through another week! During the second week, you have prayed together, you have connected over pillow talk, you have learned how not to fight and have made a commitment to fight fair, you have made a proper apology, you have performed random acts of kindness for your loved one, and you have enjoyed or scheduled a date night. Week two has been amazing! This week has been full of challenges that require you to step outside of yourself, to humble yourself, and to enhance the love and intimacy with your loved one.

Today, I challenge you to review week two. I encourage you to take this time to reflect on how the second week went for YOU. Are you still having fun? Have you felt challenged? Remember, if you find yourself struggling with a day challenge, don't give up; just keep practicing. Again, I don't expect you to gain all of this overnight. The day challenges are short-term goals. The long-term goal is to incorporate the day challenges into your life and into your relationship every day. The long-term is you *living* the daily challenges, not just *doing* the daily challenges.

If there is something about a particular challenge that makes you feel good, then do more of it. If there are parts of a challenge that are difficult for you, explore them and be honest with yourself about your findings. We are halfway through the challenges. If you have made it this far, I applaud you, I thank you, and I want to see you at the finish line in two weeks. If you have missed a few days, that's okay, too. Forgive yourself, and pick up where you left off. If you are just now joining us, welcome! We are happy that you are here and ready to love better!

The Love Challenge Facebook page, 30 Day Love Challenge is a great place to share what about The Love Challenge makes you feel good and what has been difficult for you. Thank you all so very much for pressing on! I pray that your week is full of grace.

Say It with a Song

DAY 15

Melissa Dumaz

Today, I challenge you to make a playlist for your loved one. Do you remember the good old days of making mixtapes or CDs with your favorite music as gifts for friends or significant others? Well today, you are revisiting this classic gift giving exchange. Sometimes, the best way to express exactly what you feel for someone is through a song. Today, I challenge you to find at least five songs that express your feelings to your loved one. Once your playlist is created, set aside some time to play those songs and to just sit and enjoy the music together. Music is a universal language and picks up a connection where words left off. Today, let the music speak for you!

The Power of Touch

DAY 16

Melissa Dumaz

Today, I challenge you to engage in the power of touch with your loved one. Taking the initiative to reach out and touch your loved one is a great way to communicate love (and it does not have to be sexual).

Touch strengthens relationships and enhances bonding between two people. Turn up the tactility in your life by initiating a hug or kiss, giving a pat on the back, holding hands while watching a movie, offering a massage, playing footsies under the table, giving a back rub, touching your loved ones arm or leg while driving, and rubbing their head or neck. Physical contact is precious, especially in an age where much of our time is spent texting, emailing, and living in our own little virtual world.

Studies show that touch can help lower stress, manage pain, and improve the health of mind and body at least in part, by releasing "love hormones" such as oxytocin. Touch is also a form of non-verbal communication, which is just as important as verbal communication and can be used to express joy, love, and gratitude. Not everyone enjoys the same type of touch, so modify your affection to fit your loved one's comfort.

Be sure to add a dosage of touch to your day! Remember, if you're already doing this with your loved one, today is the day you do more of it or challenge yourself to do it differently.

Appreciation List

DAY 17

Melissa Dumaz

Today, I challenge you to create an Appreciation List. Make a list of at least ten things you appreciate about your loved one. Study this list and use it as a vehicle to appreciate your loved one's positive qualities more often. Once your list is complete, commit it to heart and keep it in a safe place.

We all like to feel appreciated, and it doesn't feel good when our efforts go unnoticed. Over time, it can be damaging in a relationship when two individuals do not show appreciation for one another. Your new Appreciation List will now become your go-to list when you need a quick reminder of all the things you appreciate about your loved one. I double-dare you to read this list when you're mad at your loved one, and take note of how you feel afterward!

Today, you are focusing on a written list of things that you appreciate about your loved one. However, here's some bonus information: *spoken* praise and appreciation are also great ways to express love. The more you express appreciation for your loved one's special strengths, the more profound your appreciation will be.

Appreciation List Delivery

DAY 18

Melissa Dumaz

Today, I challenge you to go back to the Appreciation List you wrote yesterday, make a copy of it, and give it to your loved one (and no, this does not include email, text, or social media). Simply hand write or type a copy of the list you wrote yesterday, and give it to your loved one. You can either deliver it directly, mail it, or leave it somewhere they are likely to find it.

Yesterday, the focus was the creation of the Appreciation List along with studying and sowing that list deep into your heart. You have now had an opportunity to remember at least ten things that you appreciate about your loved one. Take today to remind your loved one what you appreciate about them. Life has a way of keeping everyone busy, but it's essential to make time to notice and acknowledge each other's efforts.

I understand it's easy to get settled into routines, but do not let another day go by without reinforcing your love for your significant other. They want to know that you're thinking of them, that you care, and that you appreciate them. Please

The Love Challenge

remember to show and express your appreciation with an open heart. Whatever it is your loved one needs, that is what you should be doing to show your love. Do not give anything to your loved one begrudgingly.

Give a Gift

DAY 19

Melissa Dumaz

Today, I challenge you to make or purchase a gift for your partner. While it can be extravagant if that's what you want, it does not have to be expensive to be meaningful. It can be simple and creative, yet thoughtful. Gift giving is a symbol of love and affection. A gift from you can be a visual expression and reminder of your love for your significant other. Homemade gifts, food, and flowers are effective ways of expressing your affection. Your time is also a valuable gift to give. Whatever you decide to give, be creative!

Gift giving is an act of altruism. Give with an open heart. Give without the expectation of something in return. Give as an expression your love. Your gift does not have to be elaborate. Let your loved one know that it is a "just because, no occasion" gift. Cheers to being altruistic!

Delete Your Records

DAY 20

Melissa Dumaz

Today, I challenge you to delete your records of your loved one's wrong-doings and to stop score keeping. In relationships, we have the tendency to calculate who has done what. We often complain about what our significant other is lacking and tend to overlook what we are lacking. When you start having a conversation about all the things your loved one is not, STOP yourself and change your focus.

It is easy to tally up all the things you are contributing to the relationship and to forget about all the things your loved one is doing as well. A score-keeper says or thinks things such as "I went to the store, so you have to clean up the kitchen." A score-keeper complains about the amount of time they spend cleaning the house, but overlooks the amount of time their loved one spends managing the family's finances. Score-keepers may say things such as, "Why do I always have to be the one to...? Or "I'm the only one around here who bothers to..."

The Love Challenge

All of us make mistakes. We do not always do the right thing. May all of us be reminded that love does not keep score, harbor bitterness, or seek revenge. As my pastor, Donald Bell, Sr., said, "Love math requires you to give more than you receive." Today, let go of your scorecard and embrace the fact that your love math is not going to be perfectly packaged with even numbers. Yesterday, you were challenged to create and give. Today, you are challenged to delete your records, throw away your scorecard, and give, give, give. When you are focused on giving to your loved one, there is no time to see deficiency or to keep tally.

Love Challenge Reflection: Week #3

DAY 21

Congratulations, you have made it another week! Today completes week three of The Love Challenge. During the third week, you have been challenged to communicate your love through song and touch, to create and share a list of qualities you appreciate about your loved one, and to delete your records of past wrong-doings. Week three has been full of love challenges that have asked you to be less selfish and to truly pour into your loved one.

Today, I challenge you to review week three. I pray that you have used this time to practice the many ways that you can love your significant other, and that you have found new ways to enhance your connection. Which exercises have truly challenged you this week? Did you throw in the towel, or did you press on?

You may have realized by now that this past week has been full of giving in some form or another. During week three, you have given your loved one a playlist, special touch, a list of things you appreciate, a gift, and a fresh start by deleting records and

The Love Challenge

scorecards. One thing I think we can agree on is that love requires a lot of giving, and that giving can be found in many ways.

The challenges from week three have encouraged you to practice and explore many ways to give. The long-term goal is for you to give so much love to your significant other that the many ways of giving love become innate, defying our selfish nature. Your loved one's cup should always be full. Take each challenge from last week, and simply wake each day with a new way to give love. When you find yourself tallying up all the love you have given, it means you're not giving enough. You should be giving so much love that you don't have enough numbers to keep tally any longer.

As mentioned in previous weeks' challenges, you should continue to practice the parts that are difficult for you and do more of the things that you find easy! You can also find the support of other readers along this journey with you over at The Love Challenge Facebook page, 30 Day Love Challenge.

Thank you for sticking with The Love Challenge! You have one more week to go. I pray that your week is full of love and giving.

Love Language

DAY 22

Today, I challenge you to identify your loved one's love language and to begin practicing it, so that you may learn to speak it fluently. A love language is simply a way to express love to others. Outlined by author Gary Chapman, the five languages are: words of affirmation, acts of service, receiving gifts, quality time, and physical touch.

Words of affirmation are communicated through compliments and encouragement. Acts of service involve doing something that you know your loved one would like you to do. Receiving gifts includes symbols of love like flowers, candy, and handmade gifts. Quality time consists of giving your loved one your undivided attention. Physical touch is defined by making love, hugging, kissing, and physical affection.

The challenges you completed last week prompted you to express love to your significant other with each of the five love languages. These exercises provided you the space to express love using all of the love languages, exploring and practicing a new one each day.

I encourage you to identify which one resonates the most with your loved one. Once you identify it, remember it and use it. Fill your loved one's cup by speaking their language fluently, often, and seamlessly.

One of my favorite books about identifying love languages is, *The 5 Love Languages* by Dr. Gary Chapman. I highly recommend reading it and inviting your loved one to read it as well (the audiobook is a great road trip companion). The love languages quiz is a great starting point for learning more.

It's not unusual for people to communicate through multiple love languages. Your loved one may have a primary language and some additional secondary languages. Take a few minutes each day to identify your loved one's needs and try to meet those needs using their love languages as your vehicle.

Faithfulness

DAY 23

Melissa Dumaz

Today, I challenge you to be faithful to your loved one. To be faithful is to be loyal and constant. Faithfulness is doing what you are called to do, even when you don't feel like doing it, and in relationships, that means doing what your loved one wants or needs, even when you don't feel like it. I challenge you to be faithful in all ways with your loved one. Be faithful in your roles as a spouse, a parent, and a friend.

What is your role in your relationship with your loved one? If you are not sure of your role, now is the time to identify it. Once you know your role and have agreed to it, you are responsible for walking in it. Are you the financial leader in your relationship, the chef, the house cleaner, the prayer warrior? Whatever and whoever you are in your relationship, I challenge you to be faithful in that position and to be faithful to your word. If you tell your loved one you are going to do something, do it! Life happens, and it's ok to sometimes have to change your word. I just ask one thing: be sure to go back and let your loved one know what has changed, why, and what the new word will be.

Just like many others, I have always thought that being faithful in a relationship meant not engaging in outside affairs. Life has taught me that faithfulness goes beyond outside affairs. Faithfulness is about doing what God has called me to do in all aspects of my life, especially with my loved one. Let's be honest, we all slack in some areas. However, today, I am challenging you to get back on track and get back to being faithful in all you do and say in your relationship with your loved one.

If you are unfaithful in your relationship and have been engaging in outside affairs, I encourage you to pause The Love Challenge, recommit yourself to your loved one today, and seek out help for you and your loved one from a licensed mental health professional.

Team Us

DAY 24

Melissa Dumaz

Today, I challenge you to begin the process of team building with your loved one. Yesterday, you were challenged to commit to faithfully fulfilling your role in your relationship. The next step is to focus on building. You and your loved one are a team, and in order to be an effective team, you must see you and your loved one as a unified "us" and not as a separate "me and you." When you are a team, you play for the same side, have common goals, remain faithful to your position, and operate as a cohesive unit. You share expectations for accomplishing the same task. An effective team trusts one another, supports one another, and at the same time respects one another's individual differences.

A few key factors to building a team with your loved one are commitment, communication, and collaboration. Commitment ensures that you both want the same thing, even if that same thing is simply wanting each other. Ask each other, do you want to build together? Communication is important in every relationship. Are you willing to communicate clearly and honestly with your loved one? Please recall what you learned in the Day 2 Love Challenge,

The Love Challenge

Speak Words of Love, and be mindful of speaking in love as you communicate. Collaborate with your loved one and work together to problem solve and remain faithful in your role and responsibilities of your relationship. Cooperate to establish and meet your relationship goals effectively. Yes, you and your loved one have specific roles within your relationship, and yes, you are to be faithful to those roles. However, as a team member on a team, you also step in when and where needed. Stepping in is not the same as overstepping or taking over something that your loved one is handling. Stepping in means that when your loved one needs help, you are there to lend a hand as needed.

Work together and go for the win! Just as a relay race passes the baton from one teammate to the next, do your part on your team. Begin today's challenge by replacing "I" with "we," "mine" with "ours," and "me" with "us." Once you've established US, move forward with team building. One of my favorite series, called Spiritual Partnership, from my Pastor, Donald Bell, Sr., describes partnership as "common goals for the common good commonly defined commonly executed consistently over time through change and circumstance." What are you building with your loved one?

Remember When We Met

DAY 25

Melissa Dumaz

Today, I challenge you to remember when you met your loved one. Reminisce about that moment, that time, those thoughts, those feelings, and that place where you met. Take some time to think back to the start of your relationship. Those memories keep you in love, bring you a smile, and make you fall in love all over again.

In the hustle and bustle of everyday life, it's easy to lose touch with all of those happy feelings you had at the beginning of your relationship. Remembering your first meeting with your loved one can reignite your early feelings of eager enjoyment and bring back those happy feelings. Remember the excitement of getting to know each other? Remember that chemistry? Let's get back to that enthusiasm and keep the momentum going!

I pray that your heart has been filled with love, blessings, and joy. Peace.

Bring Chivalry Back

DAY 26

Melissa Dumaz

Today, I challenge you to bring chivalry back. Now that you've had the opportunity to reminisce and get back to those happy feelings of first meeting your loved one, let's talk about chivalry. Chivalry is simply courteous behavior and includes courage, honor, loyalty, and consideration for your loved one. Somewhere along the way throughout a relationship, being courteous to one another tends to fall by the wayside. Today, I challenge you to bring chivalry back and to enhance it.

Make each other first in your lives. When was the last time you held hands with your loved one? When is the last time you danced together? (Dancing at home together counts too!) Be loyal with one another, keep your word, and show respect. Only make promises you can keep, compliment each other, show signs of affection in private and in public, and express your feelings out loud. Men: open doors for your woman, let her go first when entering a room, pull out her chair, let her order first, share your umbrella, walk on the outside of the sidewalk, and give her your coat when it's cold. Women: treat him to lunch or dinner sometimes, explore ways to woo him, verbally thank him for his chivalrous ways, and after he opens your car door and let's you inside the car, it's ok to reach over and open his door too. There are many acts of chivalry, but use this as a starting place.

Chivalry goes a long way. Let's get back to all of those wonderful things we did for and said to our loved one in the beginning. Today, pick up where you left off and treat your loved one like the person you fell in love with when you first met. Don't allow a busy life, excuses, and complacency to stop you from making the effort to be courteous, day in and day out.

Mission Statement

Day 27

Melissa Dumaz

Today, I challenge you to create a mission statement with your loved one. If you have children, I challenge you to create a family mission statement. A mission statement is a summary of your family's values and defines what your family is, why it exists, it's reason for being, and what you value. As author Stephen Covey describes it, "a family mission statement is a combined, unified expression from all family members of what your family is all about—what it is you really want to do and be—and the principles you choose to govern your family life."

What do you value in your relationship? What does your family value? What do you want your relationship and your family to be like? A family mission statement lays out a vision for your family of where you want to go together and how you want to get there. Having a shared vision—a shared sense of values and purpose—bonds us with loved ones.

I encourage you and your loved one to declare your beliefs, purpose, and goals. Start your mission statement by calling a family meeting to discuss what your family is all about, make a list of your family core values, brainstorm phrases that capture what your family is about, decide on a few big ideas, and put it all together in a mission statement. There is no right or wrong way to write your family mission statement. It can be an essay, a paragraph, or a list with bullet points.

Here are some examples (taken from *The 7 Habits of Highly Effective People* by Stephen Covey):

Example #1

- Our family mission:
- To love each other...
- To help each other...
- To believe in each other...
- To wisely use our time, talents, and resources to bless others...
- To worship together...
- Forever.

Example #2

- Our family mission:

- To always be kind, respectful, and supportive of each other.

- To be honest and open with each other.

- To keep a spiritual feeling in the home.

- To love each other unconditionally.

- To be responsible.

- To live a happy, healthy, and fulfilling life.

- To make this house a place we want to come home to.

Example #3

Our home will be a place where are family, friends, and guests find joy, comfort, peace, and happiness. We will seek to create a clean and orderly environment that is livable and comfortable. We will exercise wisdom in what we choose to eat, read, see, and do at home. We want to teach our children to love, learn, laugh, and to work on and develop their unique talents.

Example #4

- Our family mission is to:

- Value honesty with ourselves and others.

- Create an environment where each of us can find support and encouragement in achieving our life's goals.

- Respect and accept each person's unique personality and talents.

- Promote a loving, kind, and happy atmosphere.

- Support family endeavors that better society.

- Maintain patience through understanding.

- Always resolve conflicts with each other rather than harboring anger.

- Promote the realization of life's treasures.

Pray over the drafting of your family's mission statement. Once your family's mission statement is written, find a place in your home to hang it. Reference it daily and modify it as needed.

Franklin Covey has a great way to get you started with your individual or family mission statement. I recommend starting on your own first using the information provided above and then filling in any gaps by using Franklin Covey's Mission Statement Builder.

I pray that you and your family are guided in drafting a mission statement that aligns with the calling and the purpose of your life. Please feel free to share your family mission statement on my Facebook page, 30 Day Love Challenge!

Love Challenge Reflection: Week #4

DAY 28

Congratulations, you have made it through the final week! During the fourth week, you have been challenged to speak your loved one's Love Language, to be faithful, to build a team, to reminisce about the day you met, to bring chivalry back, and to create a mission statement. Week four has been full of love challenges that have asked you to recover, recoup, and rebuild.

Today, I challenge you to review week four. Continue to practice the many ways that you can continue to enhance the love between the two of you and rebuild the love as needed. How are you doing with The Love Challenge? Which exercises have challenged your love? Which challenges have encouraged you to grow?

This is the time to bring back the joy your relationship deserves, recover from anything that is not in-tune with your relationship, and to rebuild. Rebuilding with your loved one does not necessarily imply that something is broken. Rebuilding can also look like tearing down behaviors, thoughts, and feelings that do not enhance the love in your relationship. Rebuilding is strengthening your foundation and establishing new ways to express love. Now that you are recovering, recouping, and rebuilding, you are going to lay new bricks on which to continue building your love. The first brick is your mission statement, and the upcoming final challenges will assist in the rest of the construction.

Remember to continue practicing the parts of The Love Challenge that truly push you and to do more of the parts that flow effortlessly. Self-improvement is good; relationship-improvement is great.

Thank you for your commitment to The Love Challenge; you've come a long way! As we enter our final days of challenges, I pray that you receive improvement in your relationship. I pray that you are transforming to love great and to be loved greatly.

Your Vision, Your Goals

DAY 29

Melissa Dumaz

Today, I challenge you to discuss your life goals with your loved one and write them down. Have you completed your mission statement from the Day 27 Love Challenge? As the definition of what your family is, why it exists, its reason for being, and what you value, your mission statement is the first step in your rebuilding process. The next step is establishing your goals. I encourage you to discuss and write your individual, relationship, and family goals for this year and next year.

When you know what you want to achieve, it helps to focus improvement in that specific area. The end of the year is a great opportunity to reflect upon how the year went and the changes you desire for the upcoming year. Discussing and setting your goals together can truly build love in your relationship. Goals can drive you and your loved one forward, provide clarity and focus, hold you accountable, and push you to be your best.

You want your goals to be specific, measurable, attainable, relevant, and time-bound. Here's a formula that you can use to discuss and write your goals with your loved one: S.MA.R.T. Goals.

Specific. A specific goal clarifies the who, what, when, where, why, and how. For example, "I want to communicate better with my significant other," is a general goal. A more specific goal would be, "I want to use I-Statements with my loved one, so I can appropriately express my feelings with them."

Measurable. A measurable goal will help to track your progress. For example, "I am going to use an I-Statement at least one time per day," provides a concrete way to measure your goal.

Attainable. An attainable goal is realistic. In this area, you have to be honest with yourself about your limitations; however, you also have to be open and willing to push and stretch yourself in ways you never have before. Setting a goal to propose to your significant other tomorrow, when you two currently are not on speaking terms, may not be a realistic goal. A realistic goal for this scenario would be to get back on speaking terms with your loved one and resolve your current conflict.

Relevant. A relevant goal matches your needs and adds to your life's vision. For example, "I am going to purchase and read The Love Challenge to begin to increase the love in my relationship with my significant other."

Time-Bound. A time bound goal has a due date. Goals with a due date keep you on track and hold you accountable. For example, "In 30 days I will complete the The Love Challenge and tell my friends and family all about the book."

Be sure to write your goals in the positive (things you want to accomplish rather than avoid), prioritize goals based on where you want to start first, break the larger goals down into smaller goals, track your progress, and reward yourself as needed. Be mindful to keep your rewards aligned with your goals. For example, rewarding yourself with a large purchase item because you met your goal to pay off your credit cards may not be a reward that's consistent with your big picture goals.

You can also include friends and family in this process. At the beginning of every year, my husband and I host a Couple's Vision Board Party. We invite our friends over with their significant others and provide all the supplies for the making of a vision board, along with appetizers and cocktails. We do ask that our friends and their loved one discuss their goals prior to the event and come prepared to put them on their vision board. The event is a fun-filled night with liked-minded couples. We laugh, eat, and drink together, and create and share our vision boards with one another. It's always a great way start to our year and to find accountability partners!

A vision board is any sort of board on which you display images and words that represent whatever you want to be, do, or have in your life. It helps you to clarify, concentrate, and focus on specific life goals. One of the best parts of having a vision board is hanging it. We hang our vision board somewhere in our home that grants us access to looking it at every single day, which helps us reach our goals. Pray about where your life is headed next and what goals should be on your vision board.

COMMITMENTS

DAY 30

Today, I challenge you to identify and write down your relationship commitments. In the past few days, you have focused on building your relationship up by creating a mission statement and writing out goals. Now it's time to identify and write your commitments; your pledge or dedication to something specific within your relationship.

I pray that The Love Challenge has assisted you in loving your loved one better, and that is has invited your loved one to love you better. I pray that The Love Challenge has opened your eyes and your heart to the blind spots in your relationship, in a way that drives you to enhance your love. With your new eyes and heart, I am challenging you to make new commitments in your relationship. I encourage you to identify any Day Challenges that were difficult for you, that transformed you or your loved one, or that made you or your loved one feel good, loved, or at peace in your relationship. I challenge you to identify at least four commitments for your relationship for this year.

Your mission statement defines what your family is, why it exists, it's reason for being, and what you value. Your goals are desired results that you envision. Your commitments will be your pledge, your dedication to get you to your goals and to fulfill your mission. For example, if your goal is to lose weight, then you must commit to eat healthy, workout, and drink more water. In this particular Day Challenge, I am looking for you to focus more specifically on commitments for your relationship. For example, one of the commitments that my husband and I are going to make is to have more date nights. We have date nights at home, but we need more date nights outside of the home. As a couple, we are committing to have a date night outside the home at least one time per month. Personally, I am committing to speaking my husband's love language more fluently. What are you committing to in your relationship?

Once you identify your commitments, write them down! Putting your commitments in writing creates a contract between you and yourself. The same goes for goals. Once your commitments are in writing, share them with your loved one. Sharing your commitments with someone else allows the both of you to become accountability partners. You may start your commitments very simply with, *I commit to…* Make your commitments fun, keep them realistic, and, most importantly, saturate them in love.

Let's Celebrate Love

DAY 31

Congratulations, you have made it to the end of the Love Challenge! Today, we celebrate. Whether you completed all 30 challenges or only a few, you have a good reason to celebrate.

Today, I challenge you to celebrate your love with your loved one. Tonight, I want you to smile, laugh, dance, toast, and love out loud. Open your heart and allow the love to flow in and out. We are ending this challenge by celebrating love and starting a new year by celebrating love. Cheers!

My husband and I completed The Love Challenge when I first penned it. During that time, I shared my progress, my experiences, and even my difficulties with my readers. I pray that you will share yours too. You can join the 30 Day Love Challenge on Facebook and share your journey there.

Please feel free to share your experiences with the daily challenges on your social media pages, to encourage your friends and family to join. Use hashtags #ChallengeYourLove and #LoveChallengeByMel to share your journey.

Melissa Dumaz

Reflections of the Love Challenge

When I thought of The Love Challenge, I had my own relationship in mind. I wanted to be more creative in finding ways to express love and gratitude with my husband. One Sunday evening, I started jotting down ideas about how to express love, and as I looked over my list, I realized that others may benefit from the information. At that time, I had about 10 things on my list and decided I would share the info on my blog as a "Challenge," for others to join in and express love in their own relationship.

I knew I wanted the Challenge to be at least thirty days (studies show that a habit can be formed in 21-30 days); however, I did not have thirty days' worth of material. During that brainstorming period, God told me to just write and that He would guide me along the way. So, I did just that… I wrote! I created my list and each day wrote to the topic of the day. I allowed the order of the list for The Love Challenge to flow naturally from making the commitment to do the challenge, to verbally expressing love and gratitude, to doing and saying loving and gracious things in your relationship, to spending quality time together, to ending in a weekly review, and of course, to a celebration.

The Love Challenge grew from my personal experience as a woman, wife, mother, sister, friend, and therapist, but the wisdom of The Love Challenge was guided by God. I had three goals with The Love Challenge: (1) explore more creative ways to express love and gratitude to my husband, (2) share the Good News with others who would like their love to grow, (3) provide information that would transform at least one person's heart and enhance the love in their relationship. All it takes is one person to make a commitment to change, and those changes can shift the entire relationship in a positive direction. No relationship is perfect, but I pray that The Love Challenge has made some relationships better!

How was The Love Challenge for you? If you haven't already reached out, I would like to hear from you. As the author of The Love Challenge, I was excited, eager, and anxious to share. The anxiety stemmed from my commitment to write and share with my blog audience daily while I still maintained order in my marriage, family, and home. Fortunately, in that commitment, the only thing I sacrificed was sleep. Initially, I thought it was my time that was sacrificed, but I now realize that my time was given, not sacrificed. As a participant in The Love Challenge, some days were easier than others, but each day was filled with intention. When I stay focused on my love for my husband, I have little to no time to live in the lack.

I received great feedback and declarations from others about their experiences with The Love Challenge, and I am happy to hear that others have been blessed by it. The personal statements shared with me have been a reminder to continue to write, not for my glory, but for God's glory. Thank you to each and every one of you!

Declarations

When I originally shared The Love Challenge with my blog audience, there was a nice mix of married, dating, and single individuals who contacted me and expressed interest in participating. During that time, one of my friends, who we'll call AJ, shared that she was looking forward to The Love Challenge, and that my post about it was "right on time!" AJ contacted me after The Love Challenge to share her experience. Here's what she said:

"After two babies my relationship has been like a roller coaster. Mostly downhill and we had even been playing with the idea of counseling (I say playing because we haven't gone). To be honest I was almost at the point of walking away. It seemed like my next step if we didn't do something quick! Anyhow I think your love challenge was AMAZING! It gave me a lot to think about with my own actions. I shared a couple of links with my boyfriend and we would discuss topics. Although I couldn't commit to every single challenge, they were door/eye opening challenges. I think the apologizing, how to argue and the love languages were big for us. Since the new year our interaction with each other has turned all the way around. It's peaceful at home and we both actually want to be here. Not to say all of our issues are fixed and I still believe we could both use counseling, but I do feel the challenge helped. So thank you for sharing your challenge with the world.

"It's hard to let the world know your relationship is failing and the shame that comes along with being a 'baby momma' makes me feel like such a failure; not to mention all of the judging that comes along with it. We got so much pressure for not getting married 1st; I can already hear the 'I told you so'. So yeah any help we could get I was desperate for and we surely got on the

The Love Challenge

right foot with your challenge. I just pray we continue to grow and head in the right direction."

Thank you so much AJ for being so honest and open. Thank you for walking past judgement and shame and sharing your story. I pray that your candidness to share becomes a vehicle in your relationship, for your journey of "growth and being on the right foot." I pray that you and your boyfriend continue to work for your love now so that it becomes your bliss.

Around this same time, I also received a call from a family member, who we'll call GJ. He disclosed to me that he and his wife were having some ups and downs, so he invited his wife to participate in The Love Challenge with him. GJ expressed that he wanted to be a better husband, that he wanted to make things right with his wife, and that he wanted to get his marriage "back on track." He admitted that he had done things to hurt his wife and she had done things to hurt him, but he wanted to move forward and build a brighter present and future for his family.

GJ shared how The Love Challenge helped him and his wife open up their lines of communication with one another. On Day 8, Let Us Pray, he and his wife prayed together for the first time in their relationship. That night, they prayed together, embraced each other, lay in bed together, and held each other all night long. Things were peaceful and calm, and he said that night was the best sleep he had had in years! At this time during our phone call, my eyes were filled with tears of joy to know that he and his wife were seeking God. I am so grateful to GJ and his testimony. I pray that The Love Challenge is simply the beginning of many more nights of prayer, peace, and rest for him and his wife. Thank you GJ for sharing! God bless you and your family.

I asked GJ what he would tell other people about The Love Challenge and this is what he had to say: "When two people are truly in The Love Challenge together and make the effort to utilize every aspect of the challenge, all the small things that could be a challenge to your relationship will and can be placed aside to make your marriage or relationship flourish."

I also received a Facebook message from a dear friend who we'll call HF. He shared that he was single, but he was following along with The Love Challenge and felt inspired to share the information with his team at work. HF shared that he was supervising a team, predominately men, and that many of his team members disclosed to him that they were having challenges in their marriages and relationships. HF shared The Love Challenge with his team and, before the 30 days were up, he saw significant changes in his team. His teammates admitted to seeing improvements in communication, love, sex, and overall happiness in their relationship or marriage, and their love life improvements directly impacted their improvement at work in productivity, communication, and attitude!

When these brave individuals shared their declarations with me, I knew then that I needed to share this information with more people. Thus, a book was born.

About the Author

Melissa Dumaz, MS, LMFT

Melissa Dumaz is a Licensed Marriage and Family Therapist with over 15 years of experience in the mental health field. She specializes in guiding clients through the complexities of overcoming emotional and physical trauma, grief, and loss. Melissa is also passionate about supporting women through womanhood, pregnancy, and into life as a new mom. She finds joy in supporting women as they deal with the everyday stressors of life as a woman, wife, mother-to-be, or mother.

Melissa graduated from the University of La Verne with an undergraduate degree in Psychology and earned her master's degree in Counseling with a specialization in Marriage and Family Therapy from California State University Long Beach.

Melissa is happily married with three kids. She enjoys cooking for her family and friends, practicing photography, writing, painting rocks, and escaping to the nearest beach as often as possible in Southern California.

CPSIA information can be obtained
at www.ICGtesting.com
Printed in the USA
LVHW091021250720
661335LV00004BA/21/J